RANDOM BODY PARTS

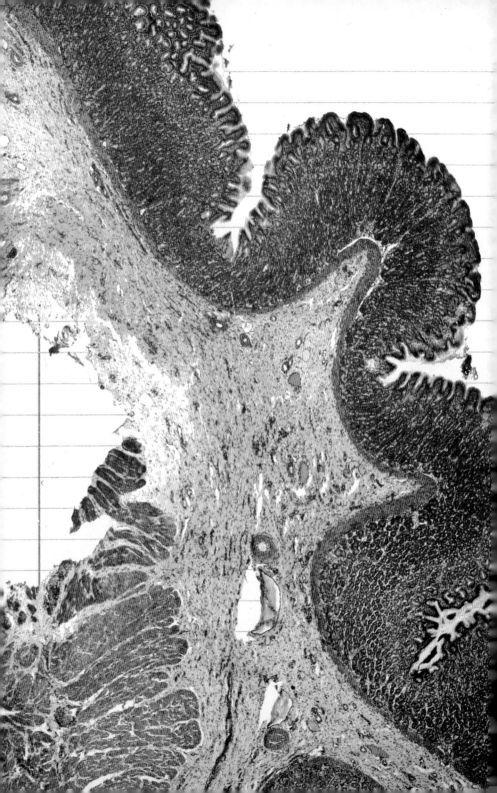

RANDOM BODY PARTS

GROSS ANATOMY RIDDLES IN VERSE

To Forest North Elementary
from Jes~ Bo 2011

WRITTEN BY **LESLIE BULION**

ILLUSTRATED BY **MIKE LOWERY**

Ω
PEACHTREE
A T L A N T A

For Caroline and Emily!
—L. B.

Published by
PEACHTREE PUBLISHERS
1700 Chattahoochee Avenue
Atlanta, Georgia 30318-2112
www.peachtree-online.com

Text © 2015 by Leslie Bulion
Illustrations © 2015 by Mike Lowery

Design and composition by Nicola Simmonds Carmack

Illustrations rendered digitally

Printed in November 2014 by RR Donnelley & Sons in China
10 9 8 7 6 5 4 3 2 1
First Edition

Library of Congress Cataloging-in-Publication Data

Bulion, Leslie, 1958- author.
  Random body parts : gross anatomy riddles in verse / by Leslie Bulion ;
illustrated by Mike Lowery.
    pages cm
ISBN 978-1-56145-737-3
  Summary: "Of course you have a body, but do you have a clue where all the
body parts you've got are found and what they do? You think you have a handle
on your anatomy, but can you handle tricky riddle poems? Come on—let's see."—
Provided by publisher.
  Audience: Ages 8-12.
  1. Human physiology—Juvenile literature. 2. Human body—Juvenile literature. 3.
Human body—Humor. 4. Riddles, Juvenile. I. Lowery, Mike, 1980- illustrator. II.
Title.
  QP37.B9275 2015
  611.002'07—dc23
                                2014006498

CONTENTS

RIDDLE
ME THIS

Of course you have a body,
But do you have a clue,
Where all the body parts you've got are found
And what they do?

You think you have a handle,
On your anatomy,
But can you handle tricky riddle poems?
Come on—let's see.

Some riddles will seem cinchy,
Some challengingly tough.
Your organs lurk between the lines
As you'll find, soon enough.

Search head to toe to locate
Each random body part.
Now keep your eyes peeled...
               Knuckle down...
                    The game's afoot...

Let's start!

READY?

LUNCHTIME

Thrice the empty pot has whined.
Thrice times thrice the cavern gapes.
The signal comes: 'Tis time, 'tis time!

In the cauldron, mix and stew
Choice ingredients for our brew:

Flesh of fowl ground into hash,
Blood of berries bled from mash,

Wheat paste wet with human spit,
Plant parts mangled bit by bit.

Grumble, grumble, roil and rumble,
Acid burn and slurry tumble.

Lumps of lard from fatted swine,
Shellfish innards laced with brine,

Spuds unearthed from mud, then fried,
Mucus oozed from deep inside,

Milk that's soured into curd—
Borborygmus roars are heard!

With a pulverizing rumble,
Churn and thrash the slushy jumble.

Your stomach, more a muscular bag than an empty pot, churns food into a thick, liquidy shake called chyme. Putting food in your cavernous mouth signals your stomach to produce strong acids and digestive juices that help break food down into nutrients your body can use. Luckily, the stomach is coated with slimy mucus so it can't digest itself! The growling sound your stomach and intestines make as they work is called borborygmus (bor/bor/**RIG**/mus).

UNEASY LIES THE HEAD
WITH NO CROWNS

First none.
Then one.
Then two.
Then four.
A full set's eight and twenty more.

Some are babyish.
Some are wise.
At mealtime they all exercise,
Which helps their roots hold strong.
They're tough.
No body part has sterner stuff.

Their workout is a nasty rout.
They slash, then gnash, then force food out.
But food bits that survive the fray,
Attack back and rot them away.

Your first baby tooth pokes through your gums when you're about six months old. By age six or so, your thirty-two permanent teeth (including four wisdom teeth) begin to push out your twenty baby teeth. Each tooth has a root below the gum line; a neck, where the tooth meets the gum; and a crown, which is the part we see. Chewing helps keep the ligaments and membranes in your gums healthy. The enamel layer on the outside of your teeth is the hardest substance in the human body.

KNOCK, KNOCK! WHO'S THERE?

You can search for lost words on my tip,
Or reveal hidden thoughts when I slip.
With my muscle-bound shove,
Tasty foods that you love,
Deconstruct on a long downward trip.

I give shape to each word that you use,
And I don't let you drown while you snooze.
All those buds on my top
Tell your brain if the slop
You are chomping is chow you should choose.

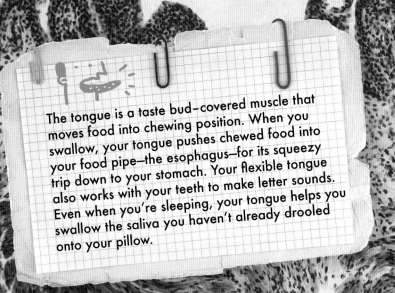

The tongue is a taste bud–covered muscle that moves food into chewing position. When you swallow, your tongue pushes chewed food into your food pipe—the esophagus—for its squeezy trip down to your stomach. Your flexible tongue also works with your teeth to make letter sounds. Even when you're sleeping, your tongue helps you swallow the saliva you haven't already drooled onto your pillow.

SONNET NUMBER FOUR

Shall I compare you to a clenched-up fist?
You are more gloppy, shaped more like a cone.
Rough handling pounds a fist upon its wrist,
But you're protected in your cage of bone.

Sometimes you are compared to two fists' size.
(Young bodies do get bigger every day.)
But soundly you'll deliver your supplies,
And lazy fists relax and fade away.

Within your rooms the hubbub never ends.
Two doors swing open wide, two others slam.
On this, the very stuff of life depends:
Fresh visitors surge in as others scram.

So long as there is breath and eyes can see,
You're hard at work—not in "asystole."

Your tireless, four-chambered heart muscle contracts about 100,000 times each day, pumping blood throughout your body: lub DUP, lub DUP. The "lub" is the sound of the doors between the two upper chambers—the atria—and the two lower chambers—the ventricles—snapping shut. The louder "DUP" is the sound of the doors banging closed between the ventricles and the two major arteries. When a heart stops contracting, that's called asystole (ay-SIS-toh-lee).

WHEREFORE ART THOU, ALVEOLI?

al VEE oh LIE
al VEE oh LIE
please tell me why
we must rely
on such small fry
to say goodbye
to carbon di-
oxide and then
how is it that you know
just when
to give us
oxygen
again?

Your lungs are spongy air exchangers made of hundreds of millions of tiny, grapelike sacs called alveoli. If all the alveoli in both of your lungs were flattened edge to edge, they'd cover a tennis court. Oxygen molecules from the air pass through the walls (only one cell thick!) of the alveoli into blood capillaries. Carbon dioxide passes from the capillaries into the alveoli and is exhaled as waste.

CRACK
THIS NUT

A wizened face
In a lofty case.

BEEP
BOOP

The brain is your body's wrinkly, three-pound control center. You're born with all of the neurons (nerve cells) your brain will ever have: about 100 billion. As you grow, move, think, learn, remember, use your senses, and experience feelings, the neurons in your brain develop new pathways to access information. How fortunate that your soft and important brain is protected by a fluid-filled, hard shell—your skull.

HMMM

QUICK AS A WINK

Gritty
if not for me—
that
is for certain.

To see
or not to see;
I
am the curtain.

Your eyelids are folds of skin, with muscles attached, that protect your delicate eyes. Every time you blink—every five seconds or so—your eyelids wash tears over your eyeballs to rinse away dirt. Oil from tiny glands between your eyelashes is added to the tears to keep the liquid from evaporating away.

THE GATEKEEPER

Oh, odors in the air are roaming,
You'll breathe them in; through me they're coming,
Reminding you of bygone days.

But pollen wafts and air is dusty,
So I make gobs of mucus disgusty,
One ripe KERCHOO! and out it sprays.

CHEERIO!

Your nose channels odor molecules deep into the back of your nasal cavity. There ten million odor sensors send messages to your brain: remember this smell? Your nose also warms and moistens air on its way to your lungs. The lining inside your nose makes mucus to trap dirt and other unwelcome particles. If the inside of your nose gets irritated, ah-ah-ah-CHOO!

THE RIVER OF LIFE

Three boats sail
Along the river of life—
A sticky situation.

A breath of wind
Where rivulets bend.
Hoist the red sails!

Many white sails gather.
Something wicked this way comes—
En garde!

A breach in the river—
Long boats glide in, then stay,
Lining the shore.

One river
With many tributaries
All shores are met.

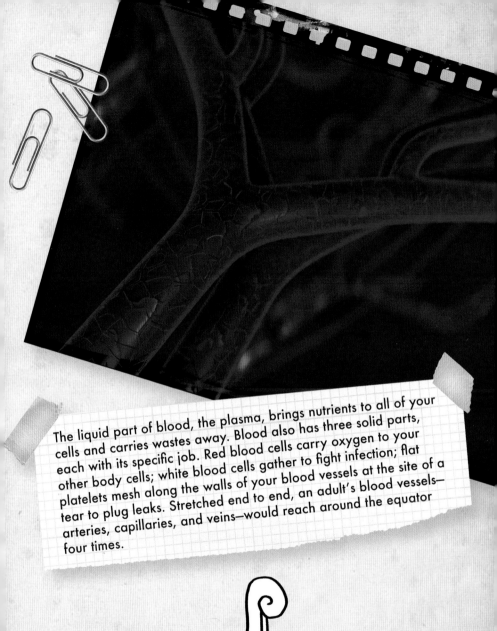

The liquid part of blood, the plasma, brings nutrients to all of your cells and carries wastes away. Blood also has three solid parts, each with its specific job. Red blood cells carry oxygen to your other body cells; white blood cells gather to fight infection; flat platelets mesh along the walls of your blood vessels at the site of a tear to plug leaks. Stretched end to end, an adult's blood vessels—arteries, capillaries, and veins—would reach around the equator four times.

WHAT BILE PART OF THIS
ANATOMY?

Three pounds of inner flush—
That's me!
I store your extra energy,
I process foodly chemistry,
In my nutrition factory.

I filter toxins night and day,
My brown-green bile trucks yuck away,
I'm bloody, muddy-red, like clay,
Three cheers for me—
Hep hep hooray!

BEEP
BEEP

The liver is your largest and heaviest internal organ. In the liver, food nutrients are made into substances your cells can use. Your blood carries these food chemicals to the heart, and from there to all of your cells. Your liver also makes liquid bile, which helps digest fats and carries food wastes out of the blood. This powerhouse organ is also in charge of storing your extra food energy.

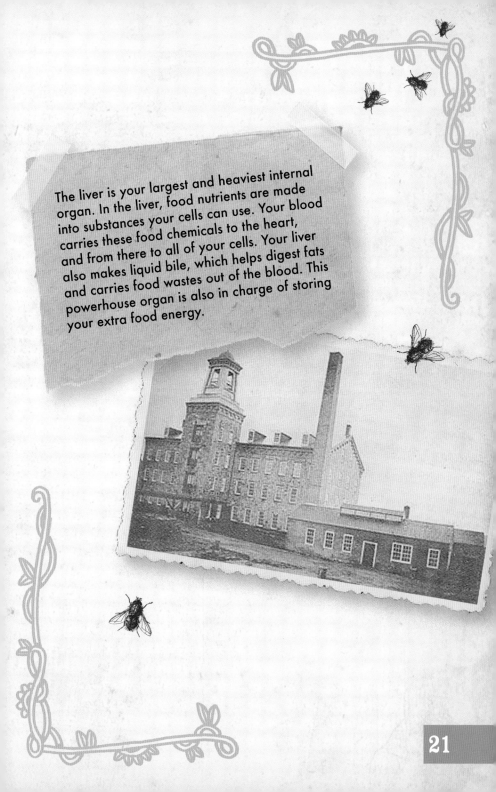

SELF-IMPORTANCE

Wolf what you will,
Swallow all kinds of swill,
If I don't add my juices, you're toast.

Without me, chewed food,
Smashed with acids and brewed
In your tum, is plain useless. No boast!

No other gland
Takes the upper hand
With protein, carb, *and* fat;

In one fell swoop
You'll have nutrient soup—
My enzymes see to that.

DING!

My other cells seep
Key hormones that keep
Your blood sugar levels on track.

Second biggest in size?
Among glands, *I'm* the prize—
That big floppy liver's a hack!

Your pancreas produces enzymes that spill into your small intestine along with the thick slurry of ground-up food from your stomach. These pancreatic juices break down proteins, carbohydrates, and fats into particles small enough to pass through your small intestine's walls and into the blood. Blood carries these small particles to the liver for further processing. Other cells in the pancreas produce important hormones to control the level of sugars in your blood.

REDUCE, REUSE, RECYCLE

The heart
is strong, the heart's
first-rate. It pumps to make
blood circulate. Blood carries food
to every cell. Blood carries oxygen
as well. Cells take blood's gifts to work
and grow, then send their wastes to
join blood's flow. Soon nutrients and
wastes are mixed. Blood's careful
balance must be fixed, or cells will
bathe in fatal brew the next time
blood comes coursing through.
But who can keep this precious
blood from fouling up with toxic
crud? Blood needs a canny
super-filter, who won't let
blood's blend tilt off-kilter.
Tuning ingredients on
the spot: Good stuff,
stay in! Out, out,
bad rot!

Inside each of your two gerbil-sized kidneys, about a million filters, called nephrons, continuously clean your blood by removing wastes your cells have produced. Nephrons also balance the amounts of salts, minerals, and water in your blood by removing some, then adding others back in. Your kidneys send wastes to the bladder to be excreted out, out—as urine.

Hidden
framework measures
two hundred and six strong—
fifty-two of them phalanges.
Handy!

Spongy
short ball-bearings
spread heavy work around,
since too much stress is never a
good plan.

Fragile
innards call for
protection from insult:
helmet, shield, and armor for a
flat fee.

Highly
irregular
to stack twenty-six rings
into a bendable, twisting
tower.

Yellow
and red marrow
in hollow logs or tucked
within stones, restock the river
of life.

Four kinds of bones protect and support your body: long bones like the femur in your thigh and the phalanges (fuh-LAN-jeez) in your fingers; short bones, like the spongy bones in your ankles; flat bones such as your ribs; irregular-shaped bones like the twenty-six vertebrae in your spine. Long bones have hollow tubes in the middle filled with yellow marrow, where fat is stored. All bones have red marrow to manufacture red and white blood cells.

GOOD RIDDANCE TO BAD BLOOD

Behind the stomach, upper left,
This gizmo (wren's nest-sized),
Is where red blood cells come to die,
And germs get neutralized.

This spongy, pulpy doodad hoards
At least a cup of blood,
Removing each red blood cell that's
An aging, worn-out dud.

Its white blood cells squelch, then remove
Bacterial invaders.
They battle every virus like
Infection Caped Crusaders.

This power worker scours blood,
All night and all day through.
Yet most folks overlook it—
I don't think that's fair.
Do you?

Your spleen sits like a jaunty little cap tipped behind the rounded, top curve of the stomach. The spleen's red pulp destroys old red blood cells and returns iron to your blood. The white blood cells, from the spleen's white pulp, surround and destroy bacteria and viruses to fight infection.

THESE MAKE SENSE

Our back end's plumpy.

> We're all thin.

We wake to work
when light comes in.

> We're on the job
> for dim night vision.

We're the masters
of precision.

> We all stand up against the wall,
> inside our gooey jelly ball.

We're into red and green and blue.

> Black and white is what we do.
> And shapes of things—

More light! More light!

> It's good.

A thousand times good night!

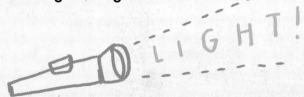

Light receptor cells—rods and cones—line the back of the inside of your eyeball, called the retina. You have nearly twenty times more rods than cones. Rods detect shapes, and shades of black and white in low light. Each cone cell needs bright light to detect fine detail and just one color: red, blue, or green. Your brain turns the messages nerves transmit from all of those rods and cones into "seeing."

THROUGH THICK
AND THIN

All that shivers deep within,
Like liver, kidney (and its twin),
Intestine, brain, and sharp-edged shin,
Must have this cloak to swaddle in,
This organ with the discipline,
To keep muck out and fluids in,
Protecting all through thick and thin,
Producing helpful melanin,
In swatches where the sun has been.

The largest organ in your body is your skin. Skin protects your inner organs from damage, regulates your body temperature, keeps germs and water outside, and keeps important body fluids *inside*. Among its many other talents, skin produces brown melanin, a chemical that absorbs some of the sun's harmful UV rays.

O EXCELLENT MOTION!

In human bodies, who can pull their weight?
To raise your hand and answer, flex your deltoid.
Who's paired to work in turns and alternate?
In human bodies, who can pull their weight?
The gluteus maximus is the all-time great.
No guess? Then shrug trapezius and rhomboid.
In human bodies, who can pull their weight?
Now, raise your hand and answer—flex your deltoid!

Skeletal muscles account for two-fifths of your total weight. Most skeletal muscles come in pairs that pull on bones to create movement and keep your body stable. When your brain sends the message: raise my hand, your deltoid (DEL-toyd) contracts, pulling up the long bone in your upper arm. When you put your hand down, the latissimus dorsi (lah-TIH-sih-muss DOOR-sigh) in your back contracts, while the deltoid relaxes.

Whispered waves echo echo echo
into a funnel
into a tunnel
where the head of a drum
stretches and vibrates,
hitting the handle
of a delicate hammer
that knocknocknocks
on an elfin anvil
that rattles a slender stirrup
against the tissue-thin dam
of a spiraling, inner sea
whose watery surges
bend bristly bundles
that send a series of signals
to decipher
the secret.

WHISPER WHISPER

Your outer auricles (outer ears) collect sound waves and funnel them along ear canals to the eardrums. Your eardrums vibrate. This motion is passed along by three tiny, tool-shaped middle ear bones in turn. When the last bone jiggles against the door to your inner ear, the inner ear fluid sloshes, causing sensitive hair cells inside to bend. Nerves connected to those hair cells translate the bending into electrical messages to your brain so you can make sense of what you're hearing.

A COMPLAINT OR THE MOST UNKINDEST CUT OF ALL

Crankildy, rankledy,
Gall bladder, diaphragm,
Ligaments, ileum—
We're in a fuss!

We're perfect subjects for
Riddlanatomies.
Someone should write crackpot
Poems about *us!*

GLOSSARY

anatomy—the science of the structure and function of an organism and its parts

arteriole—a tube-like vessel that connects a larger artery to a small capillary

artery—a large, tubular vessel that carries blood away from the heart to other parts of the body

bacterium—one of a group of single-celled organisms that live independently in soil or water, or live on or inside an animal or plant as parasites; plural: bacteria

capillary—a tiny, tube-like blood vessel that connects arterioles to venules in a network that carries blood to and from every part of the body

carbon dioxide—a colorless gas produced as a waste product by the cells of an animal

cartilage—a firm, flexible tissue that cushions bones; the outer ear and the tip of the nose are made of cartilage

circulate—follow a regular course and return to the starting point

deltoid muscle—the large muscle at the back of the shoulder that raises the upper arm when contracted, and helps move the arm backwards and forwards

BACK

diaphragm—the large, muscular partition that separates the abdominal area from the chest cavity; it helps change the volume of the chest cavity during breathing

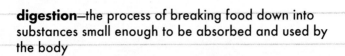

digestion—the process of breaking food down into substances small enough to be absorbed and used by the body

esophagus—the muscular tube that transports food from the back of the throat down to the stomach

enzyme—a compound, usually a protein, that speeds up a chemical reaction in an organism

gall bladder—the pear-shaped, muscular sac near the liver that stores bile for use in digestion of fats

gland—an organ or group of cells that produces a substance for use elsewhere in the body or elimination from the body

gluteus maximus—the large muscle located in each buttock that extends the upper leg and helps rotate it outward; the largest muscle in the body

hepatic vein—a vein that carries blood away from the liver

hormone—a chemical substance produced in the body that has a specific effect on another organ or group of cells

ileum—the third and last section of the small intestine; it connects with the large intestine

latissimus dorsi—a large muscle on either side of the middle of the back that lowers the arm and pulls it back when contracted

BACK

ligament—a strong tissue that connects bones or cartilage

oxygen—a chemical element (existing in nature as a gas) that most organisms need to make energy

parasite—an organism that lives all or part of its life cycle on or in a host organism, causing harm to the host

receptor cell—one of the specialized cells in an organism that responds to sensory stimulation such as light, sound, odor, heat, pressure, or flavor

rhomboid muscle—two muscles, the rhomboideus major and the rhomboideus minor, that pull each shoulder blade toward the spine and upward

toxin—a poison produced by an animal, plant, or bacterium →

trapezius—a large triangular muscle on either side of the upper-back, neck, and shoulder area that raises and lowers the shoulder, and also raises the head

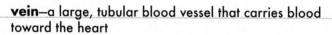

vein—a large, tubular blood vessel that carries blood toward the heart

venule—a tube-like vessel that connects a small capillary to a larger vein

virus—an infectious agent smaller than a bacteria that can only live and reproduce inside a living cell

LIKE A
COLD
VIRUS
→

AH
CH OO!

SOME PARTS OF THE HUMAN BODY

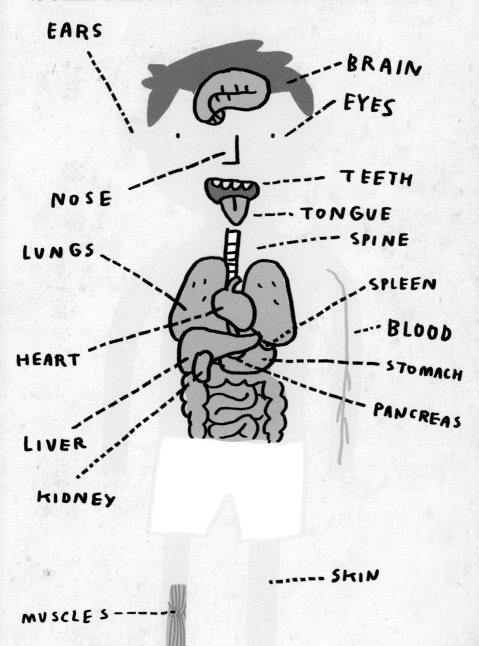

EARS

BRAIN

EYES

NOSE

TEETH

TONGUE

SPINE

LUNGS

SPLEEN

BLOOD

HEART

STOMACH

PANCREAS

LIVER

KIDNEY

SKIN

MUSCLES

POETRY NOTES:

RIDDLE ME THIS
This poem has four separate parts, called stanzas. The first three stanzas in this poem have four lines each. Lines of poetry often have a rhythm, set by the number of strong beats in the line. The first two lines in each stanza in this poem have three strong beats:

> Of **COURSE** you **HAVE** a **BO**/dy,
> But **DO** you **HAVE** a **CLUE**?

Speaking of clues, though Sir Arthur Conan Doyles's character Sherlock Holmes famously says "the game is afoot," Shakespeare wrote it first in his historical play *Henry IV, Part I*.

LUNCHTIME
This poem is written with the same rhyme pattern and number of beats, or meter, as the witches' speech in William Shakespeare's play, *Macbeth*: "Double, double toil and trouble;/Fire burn, and cauldron bubble." Imitating a well-known poem is a wonderful way to practice rhythm and rhyme in poetry. After the first three non-rhyming lines, the rest of the poem is written in couplets—two lines in a row that rhyme. What part of your body is "the cavern" in the beginning of the poem?

UNEASY LIES THE HEAD WITH NO CROWNS
This poem consists of five rhyming couplets. Many of the lines in the poem are broken into smaller sections, so it may be hard to recognize where the couplets start and stop. The title of the poem is a twist on King Henry IV's line: "Uneasy lies the head that wears a crown." The phrase "sterner stuff" means "stronger stuff," and was spoken in Shakespeare's tragedy, *Julius Caesar*.

KNOCK, KNOCK! WHO'S THERE?
Limericks have five lines. The first, second, and fifth lines rhyme and have three strong beats. The fourth and fifth lines rhyme, and have two strong beats each. The very first knock, knock joke may have been told by the porter answering the door in Shakespeare's quite serious play, *Macbeth*.

SONNET NUMBER FOUR
Sonnet Number Four is a parody (a humorous version) of "Sonnet 18," a love poem that begins "Shall I compare thee to a summer's day?" It is written in Shakespeare's typical sonnet form of three four-line stanzas, then a rhyming couplet at the end. The first and third lines in each stanza rhyme, and the second and fourth lines rhyme. Each line has five strong beats in this two-syllable rhythm soft **STRONG**:

On **THIS**, the **VE**/ry **STUFF** of **LIFE** de/**PENDS**.

WHEREFORE ART THOU, ALVEOLI?
In this free-wheeling, rhymed riddle, the title asks the reader where alveoli are, in the same way Juliet famously wonders "O Romeo, Romeo! wherefore art thou, Romeo?" in Shakespeare's tragedy, *Romeo and Juliet*.

CRACK THIS NUT
A brief, two-line rhyming poem is an epigram. This epigram riddle uses a metaphor, where one image is used to reMIND the reader of something else. People say "crack this nut" to mean "solve this difficult problem." In *Troilus and Cressida*, Shakespeare used the metaphor of "cracking a nut" to mean splitting someone's head open. Ouch!

ALAS!

QUICK AS A WINK
Hamlet's line, "To be, or not to be: that is the question," may be the most-quoted line in all of Shakespeare's plays and sonnets. In "Quick as a Wink" the line is pulled apart into a stanza, to encourage the reader to pause at the end of each very short line. It is rhymed with a second short stanza in the same rhythm pattern.

WINK!

THE GATEKEEPER
Song lyrics (the words) are poems. Writing new lyrics to an old song is another fun way to practice rhythm and rhyme. In Shakepeare's comedy *Twelfth Night*, the clown sings a song in the rhythm and rhyme pattern copied in this nose poem, that begins like this: "O mistress mine, where are you roaming?" "Roaming" and "coming" are the same rhyming pair that Shakespeare used in his poem, which is an off-rhyme, not an exact rhyme.

THE RIVER OF LIFE
The poems in this haiku-like series each have three lines, and no more than seventeen total syllables (parts of words) in each poem. As in most traditional haiku, they contain a metaphor from nature, comparing our circulatory system to a river. But none contains the traditional kigo—a phrase that tells us something about the season. When the second witch in Shakespeare's *Macbeth* says, "By the pricking of my thumbs/ Something wicked this way comes," she is letting her witch sisters know that murderous Macbeth has arrived.

WHAT BILE PART OF THIS ANATOMY?
This poem was written with two stanzas of four lines each. All four lines in each stanza rhyme. The exclamations "That's me!" and "Hep hep hooray!" are originally parts of the lines above them, but set on their own for emphasis. The title is borrowed from Romeo's question about his name and where it might be found

in his own body: "In what vile part of this anatomy/ Doth my name lodge?" He is a Montague, and his family is feuding with Juliet's family, the Capulets. This poem's first line may remind some Shakespeare scholars of the famous demand for payment of "a pound of flesh" from Shakespeare's play, *The Merchant of Venice*.

SELF-IMPORTANCE

The first two lines of each of the tercets (three-line stanzas) in this poem have two strong beats, and rhyme with each other. The third line has three strong beats, and rhymes with the last line in another tercet. This poem also uses "enjambment," which means that one line runs into the next to complete an idea.

> Without me, chewed food,
> Smashed with acids and brewed
> In your tum, is plain useless. No boast!

The often-used phrase "one fell swoop," which we use to mean several things being taken care of all at once, comes from Shakespeare's *Macbeth*.

REDUCE, REUSE, RECYCLE

A shape poem, or concrete poem, uses the printed form to tell us something important about its subject, in this case, the kidney. This poem ends with its own version of Lady Macbeth's famous line: "Out, damned spot!" which is also about cleaning blood. In her case, though, she is trying to wash the blood of the murdered king from her hands.

FIRM OF PURPOSE

THESE HANDS!

A cinquain is a five-line poem that follows this pattern: two syllables, four, six, eight, two. "Firm of purpose" is a series of cinquains, and a play on Lady Macbeth's insult to her husband, "Infirm of purpose!" when she feels he's lost his nerve after murdering the king.

GOOD RIDDANCE TO BAD BLOOD

A ballad stanza is a four-line stanza. Lines one and three have four strong beats and may or may not rhyme. Lines two and four have three beats and rhyme. Many American folk songs are written in ballad stanzas. The last line of this poem is a question, set on its own, extra line. We say "good riddance" to mean we're glad to be rid of something or someone. But Shakespeare said it first in his play *Troilus and Cressida*, and then in *The Merchant of Venice*.

THESE MAKE SENSE

"These Make Sense" is a rhyming poem for two voices. Sometimes the rods are speaking, sometimes the cones, and sometimes both speak together. The cones say "A thousand times good night!" when they don't sense enough light. This is a much less romantic use of Juliet's line than when she bids her sweetheart "a thousand times good night" from her balcony in Shakespeare's *Romeo and Juliet*. Poets often invent words, and the word "plumpy" was invented by Shakespeare.

THROUGH THICK AND THIN

This poem is written in the pattern of a note found in a golden chest in Shakespeare's *The Merchant of Venice* that begins with this statement: "All that glisters (glitters) is not gold." The poem has nine rhyming lines with four strong beats in each line. Many people say "all that glitters is not gold" as a warning that something very beautiful or inviting may not turn out so great upon closer inspection or with more experience.

O EXCELLENT MOTION!

A triolet is an eight-line poem form with only two rhyme sounds. The first line is repeated exactly as the fourth and seventh lines, and the third and fifth lines also use the same rhyme sound. The second line is repeated as the eighth line, and rhymes with the sixth.

In Shakespeare's *The Taming of the Shrew*, the fool Grumio says, "O excellent motion!" meaning "what a great suggestion!" when a group of rivals calls a truce so they can go and enjoy supper together.

FRIENDS, ROMANS, COUNTRYMEN, LEND ME YOUR AURICLES!

Free verse has no set rhythm or rhyme, other than that which the poet hears as he or she explores the images and ideas of the poem. The title of this poem is a play on the often-quoted line: "Friends, Romans, countrymen, lend me your ears!" from Shakespeare's *Julius Caesar*.

A COMPLAINT OR THE MOST UNKINDEST CUT OF ALL

A dactyl is a rhythmic word or phrase that has three parts with one strong beat: **STRONG**/soft/soft, like the word **LIG**/a/ment. The first three lines of each stanza in a double dactyl have two dactyls in a row. The fourth line of each stanza has one dactyl and finishes with one strong beat. For extra fun, the first line of a double dactyl contains two nonsense words, the second line should have the name of the subject of the poem, and the sixth line is one long word that has the rhythm and meter of two double dactyls: **RI**/ddle/a/**NA**/to/mies. People say "the unkindest cut of all" when they want to emphasize how something might hurt more in an emotional sense than in a physical or practical sense. In Shakespeare's play *Julius Caesar*, the phrase "the most unkindest cut of all" means that Brutus stabbed Caesar with a knife, but also that Caesar's feelings were hurt to know that his trusted friend Brutus would do such a thing.

FOR FURTHER INVESTIGATION:

British Broadcasting Corporation. "Human Body and Mind: The Body." www.bbc.co.uk/science/humanbody/body/index.shtml (Packed with information, interactive games, quizzes, articles and video features on a wide and deep variety of human body topics.)

Folger Shakespeare Library. "Shakespeare for Kids." www.folger.edu/Content/Teach-and-Learn/Shakespeare-for-Kids/ (A treasure trove of games, scripts, Bardian insults, and much more. A wonderful introduction to the Folger Library's magnificent collection.)

MEDtropolis. "The Virtual Body." www.medtropolis.com/virtual-body/ (Well-drawn, clear diagrams with interactive labeling and games teach how the body is put together, with narrated short diagrammatic videos in each section.)

National Geographic. "Human Body." www.science.nationalgeographic.com/science/health-and-human-body/human-body/ (Animated interactives and feature articles with signature *National Geographic* graphics and photography that combine to bring the human body up close and personal.)

Parker, Steve, and David West. *Brain Surgery for Beginners: And Other Major Operations for Minors.* Hemel Hempstead, Herts: Simon & Schuster Young, 1993. (Illustrated with accuracy and humor, this informational text provides a fun, rich, accessible view of human anatomy.)

ACKNOWLEDGMENTS:
HEARTfelt thanks to so many at Peachtree for their support, encouragement, and hours of attention to wrangling all of my random poetry parts into such a carefully designed and well-executed package. I appreciate each and every minute of your work. Never-ending thanks to my family for their love and support, and to Rubin, in particular, for his expertise and his copy of *Gray's Anatomy*.